Lily's Play[house]

Story by Jackie Tidey
Photography by Lindsay Edwards

Rigby
A Harcourt Achieve Imprint

www.Rigby.com
1-800-531-5015

"Mom," said Lily.

"I am going

to my playhouse."

"Oh no!" said Lily.

"Look at the rain."

"You cannot go
to the playhouse,"
said Mom.

Lily looked

at the big chairs.

And she looked

at the blue cover.

"The chairs can go here,"

said Lily.

"The blue cover

can go here," said Lily.

"Look, Mom," said Lily.

"Look at my playhouse."

"You can come in here, too,"

said Lily.

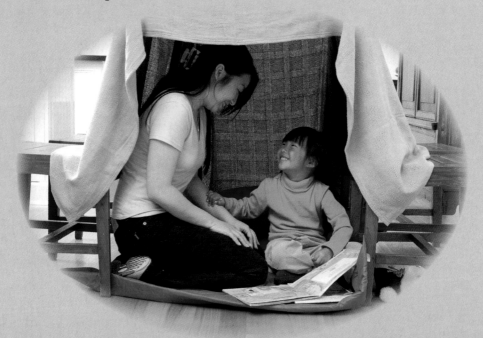